This book belongs to

_____

Ninja Life Hacks™

This book is dedicated to my children - Mikey, Kobe, and Jojo.

Confident Ninja

By Mary Nhin

Pictures by
Jelena Stupar

Over a mountain by a colorful geyser lived a ninja named Confident Ninja.

He wasn't afraid to be himself or speak up for the less fortunate.

For example...

If Confident Ninja got confused in class, he would ask for help.

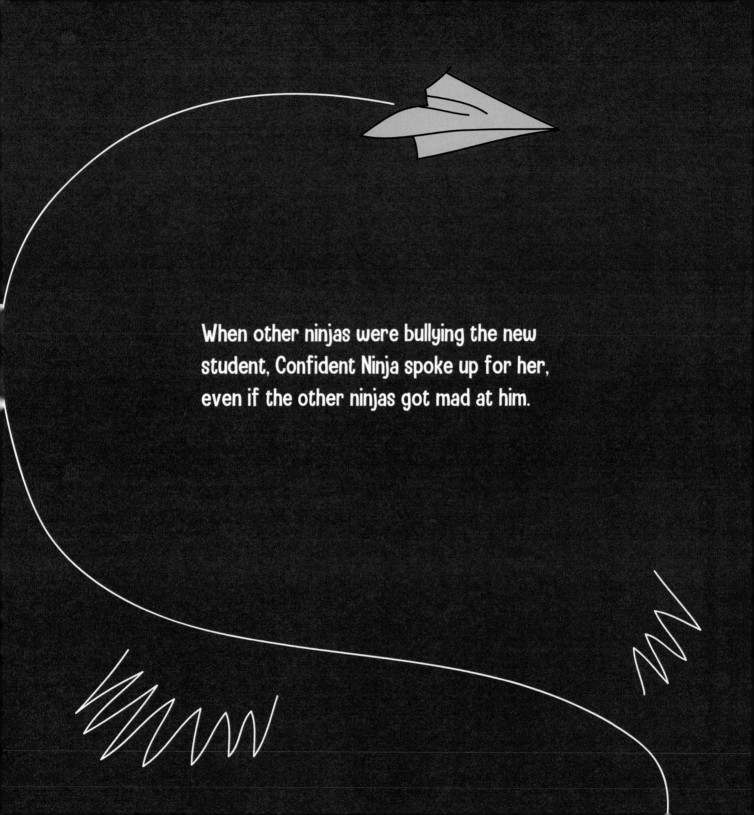

When other ninjas were bullying the new
student, Confident Ninja spoke up for her,
even if the other ninjas got mad at him.

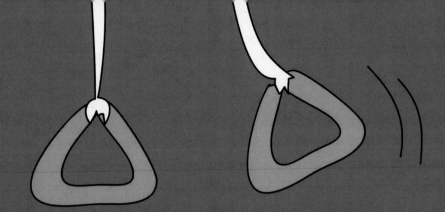

During gym class, Confident Ninja wasn't afraid
to try new things or look uncoordinated...

but it was not always like this...

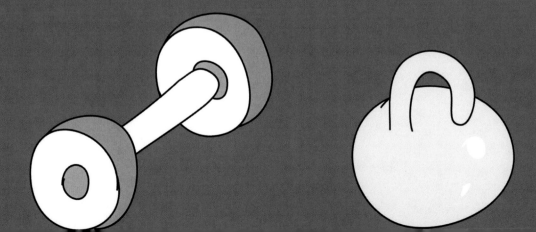

When the teacher asked for a volunteer, Confident Ninja
wanted to raise his hand, but then he decided he better not...

When he made a mistake, he would think negatively of himself.

And if he saw something that shouldn't be happening, he hesitated to say anything.

Picture yourself succeeding.

We all have an inner voice in our head. Sometimes, this voice says negative things like, *You can't do that.*

So it's good to notice when this negative voice is talking. Then, replace it with a positive thought.

One way to picture yourself succeeding is through a positive affirmations mirror. It reminds us to say one positive thing about ourselves, before we start our day. And if you believe in yourself, you're already halfway there!

Practice failing.

Did you know successful people fail many times before succeeding? J.K. Rowling was rejected by twelve different publishers before one picked up "Harry Potter."

Failing isn't bad, it's necessary. Ninjas who fail regularly but keep trying have a growth mindset. They believe they will eventually succeed.

For example, the Wright Brothers failed seven times before designing a successful airplane.

Put your goals down on paper.

Using a goal rocket chart makes it easier to accomplish your goal by allowing you to break it down into smaller steps.

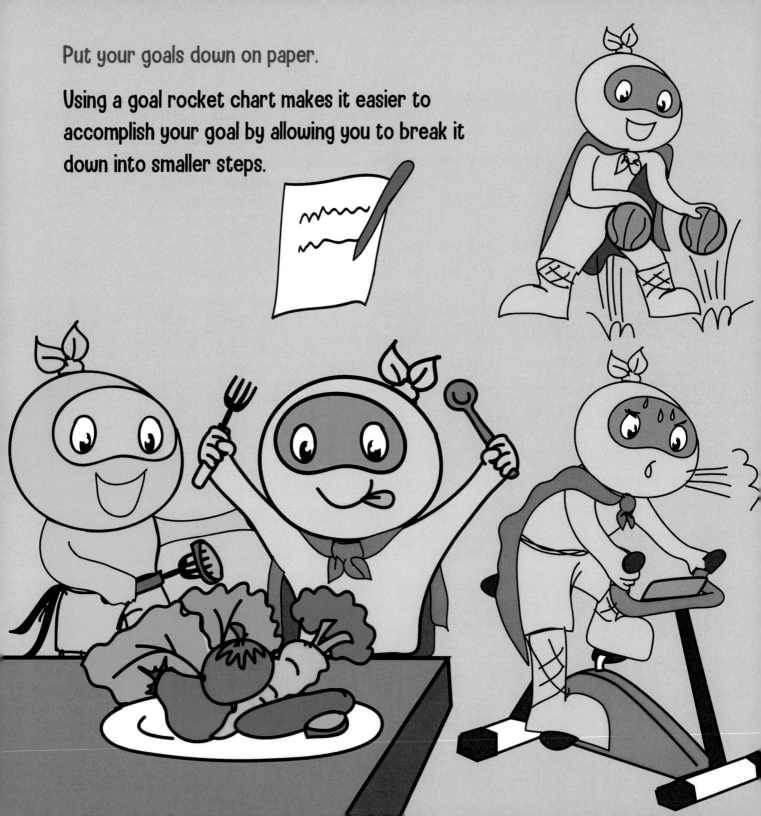

That evening, Confident Ninja wrote down his rocket goal.

He thought about the times he was kind...

and smart...

and brave.

After failing several times to make the basketball team, he decided to try again. He practiced a lot and worked really hard.

And then, guess what happened?

He made the team!!!

Remembering the Confidence Code could be your secret weapon to combat low self esteem.

Download the Positive Affirmations template for your mirror to grow your confidence today at growgrit.co

 @marynhin @GrowGrit
#NinjaLifeHacks

f Mary Nhin Grow Grit

▶ Grow Grit

Made in the USA
Coppell, TX
21 December 2020

46927433R10024